THESE
music
EXAMS

• •

Jean Harvey
Chief Examiner
of The Associated Board of
the Royal Schools of Music

First published in 1982.
This edition first published in 1994.
Reprinted 1995, 1996, 1997.
The Associated Board of the Royal Schools
of Music (Publishing) Ltd
14 Bedford Square, London WC1B 3JG

© 1994 by The Associated Board of
the Royal Schools of Music

ISBN 1 85472 757 5

Design and artwork by
Lawrence Cheung Limited, London
Printed in Great Britain by
Caligraving Limited

CONTENTS

INTRODUCTION

At the very heart of the Associated Board's work lie three convictions: first, that the arduous journey towards musical accomplishment is of great intrinsic value to all who embark purposefully upon it; secondly, that milestones enable most travellers to travel faster and further; and thirdly, that Associated Board graded examinations are the best milestones for this particular journey.

It would be neither right nor necessary to use this Introduction to argue on behalf of the first of these propositions. Almost every reader of this booklet will already be convinced of the immense educational benefits, fulfilment and joy which the development of musical skills can generate.

Milestones should not be misused. Reaching the next one is never the ultimate purpose of a journey. Their dual function is to provide an immediate goal and a measure of progress to date; and most of us need both of these at regular intervals to help us on our way. This is true irrespective of the length of journey undertaken.

The Associated Board's graded examinations have exactly these characteristics and qualities in the context of learning a musical instrument. They are the outcome of long experience and a continuing collaborative and consultative process amongst leading musicians, both teachers and performers, ensuring that each element of musicianship is well developed and accurately measured at each grade. The examinations work for everyone who wants to develop these skills, whatever their starting point, talent or length of commitment.

The purpose of this booklet – which was first published in 1982 and has been widely praised ever since – is to explain these music exams in more detail and to provide practical advice for candidates, teachers and parents. In this new edition, information is updated, descriptions of the Licentiate Diploma and Performance Assessment are incorporated and there is a new section, within General Hints for Candidates, on written examinations; the tables setting out criteria have been fine-tuned to provide a more coherent and logical framework for assessment of technical, musicianship and performance skills; and an outline plan has been added immediately after this Introduction, so that those readers who are less familiar with these music exams can have an overview of all Associated Board syllabuses and their principal features.

Richard Morris

R F M Morris
Chief Executive
25th November 1993

OUTLINE PLAN OF ASSOCIATED BOARD EXAMINATIONS

**WRITTEN (THEORY)
OR PRACTICAL
MUSICIANSHIP**

PRACTICAL

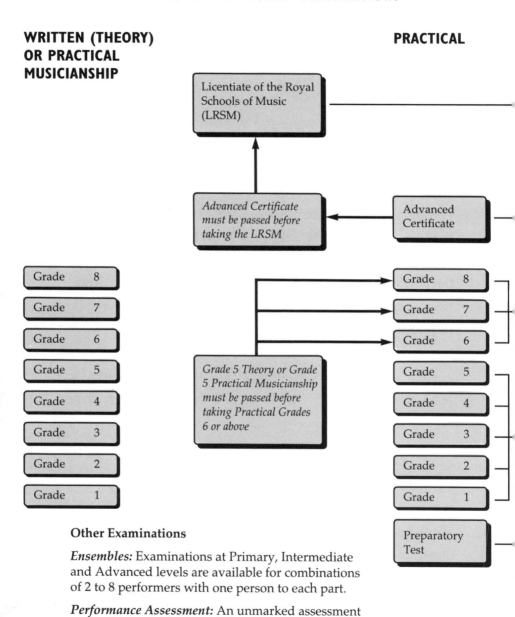

Licentiate of the Royal
Schools of Music
(LRSM)

*Advanced Certificate
must be passed before
taking the LRSM*

Advanced
Certificate

| Grade 8 |
| Grade 7 |
| Grade 6 |
| Grade 5 |
| Grade 4 |
| Grade 3 |
| Grade 2 |
| Grade 1 |

*Grade 5 Theory or Grade
5 Practical Musicianship
must be passed before
taking Practical Grades
6 or above*

| Grade 8 |
| Grade 7 |
| Grade 6 |
| Grade 5 |
| Grade 4 |
| Grade 3 |
| Grade 2 |
| Grade 1 |

Preparatory
Test

Other Examinations

Ensembles: Examinations at Primary, Intermediate
and Advanced levels are available for combinations
of 2 to 8 performers with one person to each part.

Performance Assessment: An unmarked assessment
of performance is available to adults aged 21 or over.

SYLLABUS

Part 1 is for all Branches and consists of 2 written papers, or approved course-work assessment.
Part 2 consists of one Branch selected by the candidate.

Prepared Performance
Quick Study, Viva Voce &
   Musicianship Tests

3 set pieces (Singing: 4 songs)
Scales and arpeggios, from memory
   (Singing: unaccompanied
   traditional song)
Sight-reading
Aural tests

3 set pieces (or songs)
Scales and broken chords/arpeggios from
   memory (Singing: unaccompanied
   traditional song)
Sight-reading
Aural tests

Basic exercises
Set piece (or song)
Piece (or song) of candidate's own choice
Aural tests

NOTES

LRSM: Branches available:
A: Composition
B: Music in the School Curriculum
C: Teaching (Instrumental or Voice)
D: Performance
E: Direction
F: Piano Accompaniment

Advanced Certificate: *a performance examination beyond Grade 8 and an intermediate step towards the LRSM, available in all practical subjects.*

Practical Examinations: *available for piano, organ, harpsichord, violin, viola, cello, double bass, guitar, harp, singing, recorder, flute, oboe, clarinet, bassoon, saxophone, horn, trumpet, cornet, flugelhorn, Eb horn, trombone, bass trombone, baritone, euphonium, tuba and percussion. Candidates may be entered in any grade and without previously having taken any other practical grade.*

Preparatory Test: *an unmarked assessment designed for pupils after 6-9 months' tuition. It can be used to prepare pupils for the graded Practical examinations.*

This outline plan is intended for general guidance only. Please refer to the Examination Regulations and relevant syllabuses for exact details of all examinations.

STANDARDS

From the lowest grade to the highest, it is of primary importance that a recognised reliable standard exists. In an assessment, musical awareness must be balanced and supported by technical competence: the two aspects are essentially inter-related. It is these two factors which form the starting point for the examiner's assessment. It has to be accepted that an inherently musical performance would be spoilt by technical insecurity and, conversely, a technical display without feeling would be an unmusical performance. Indeed, one could go further and say that in the anxiety which an examination can produce, technical control must be assured if extraneous circumstances are not to upset carefully prepared work and affect the musical performance itself.

From time to time, teachers and parents argue that the stumbles, slips and inaccuracy described on the mark form could not have occurred as they had heard a near-perfect performance prior to the examination, but it will happen that weaknesses, not previously revealed, will be shown up by the special circumstances of the occasion. The examiner will have to refer to such weaknesses if the overall performance is affected. These examinations are concerned with the musical development of the aspiring player. Being able to play the notes accurately and rhythmically as a basis for a good performance cannot be stressed too strongly.

It must be remembered that examiners can only assess what they hear. They will mark according to the criteria for assessment which have been the hallmark of the Associated Board's examinations since their foundation in 1889. These criteria are included on pages 28 to 32 of this booklet.

It may be possible to make quicker progress on some instruments, especially in the early stages. However, a similar standard of competence is expected on all instruments and in singing at each grade.

Candidates should not expect the same high marks to be given automatically as they go through the grades. Unless sufficient time is allowed between examinations to develop musical and technical skills, and to acquire the necessary maturity which is involved in playing the more advanced pieces, results will be disappointing. Likewise, speed of development will always vary, and results may be less good than expected unless periods of consolidation are included in the study programme.

The examinations can be taken by anyone, at any age. They are for amateurs in so far as they are intended to cover what may be learned within the first 10 years of musical development. Some candidates will complete the eight grades quickly, while others will take considerably longer and may well find that success in the higher grades will elude them. At this stage there is frequent disappointment when low marks are given, especially if there has been considerable success in earlier grades. The most common reason for this is insufficient appreciation of the maturity required in musical perception and understanding in order to play the pieces set, especially for Grades 7 and 8.

Singers need to be particularly careful to match their repertoire selection to their vocal qualities and capabilities.

TO THE CANDIDATE - WHAT YOU NEED TO KNOW

SCALES AND TECHNICAL EXERCISES

The importance of a reliable technical facility has already been stressed. One way to help ensure this is to practise scales and arpeggios daily. Such exercise promotes the physical aspects of playing: it is also a basic discipline like that required for any physical activity. It is for this reason that they are included as part of the syllabus. For wind players they will help breathing and for string players bowing control; for all, the general co-ordination required for playing an instrument will develop in proportion to the regular effort put into practice.

Candidates who play scales badly usually create unnecessary anxiety for themselves. Pianists frequently play scales too slowly. It may be helpful to aim for the recommended minimum speeds suggested on pages 24-25 of this booklet. However, these should only be treated as a guide.

AURAL

The purpose of the aural tests is to ensure that aural training is part of a musician's training, but this is a section which often produces problems for candidates. Unless regular aural training is part of learning to sing, or play an instrument, responses in these tests in the examination will be weak, especially so as you progress to the higher grades. Candidates should practise regularly to acquire listening skills before using the tests. So often there is a lack of a proper focus of listening in the pitch tests apparent from the response itself.

SIGHT-READING

Sight-reading is an indispensable asset to all musicians. It leads to quick learning and independence. It might be said that to keep going is the key to a pass mark in this section. To stop or hesitate, in order to find the correct notes, could mean a lower mark than would otherwise be the case. It is therefore wise to use the thirty seconds allowed before starting the test to find any difficult notes, to try out awkward rhythm patterns and chords.

ORNAMENTS

Candidates may use their own interpretation of ornaments although editors' suggestions are based on research and scholarship and should be treated as authentic guidelines. It is important that the musical line is undisturbed by ornamentation and that the rhythmic pulse remains steady. It is much better to use a turn or mordent rather than to try and play a complicated trill if the latter would be clumsy. If any ornament is hazardous it is wiser to omit it: the performance will not fail because of this, but obviously, a high mark will be sacrificed.

DA CAPO AND REPEATS

Da capo and *dal segno* signs should be observed although the examiner may choose to hear only a few bars. Other repeats of more than a few bars should not be played in the examination unless the examiner asks for them.

PLAYING FROM MEMORY

Extra marks are not given for playing pieces from memory in Associated Board examinations although it is a skill worth developing. The extra facility will lead to a more convincing performance. It is, however, entirely up to the candidate whether to play from memory or not.

It should be noted that singers are required to sing from memory.

MARKS AND REMARKS

By the very nature of the occasion, and the length of time allocated to the examination (especially in the early grades when pieces are short), it is not possible to include every detail of performance in the comments given by examiners. They will, however, endeavour to give encouragement. Remember the comments are there to give you, the candidate, an idea of how to improve where there are weaknesses and to encourage strengths. There is little point in giving an assessment which does not truly represent what has been heard. The amount written will vary, but the remarks will always be a record of what was heard. It is also important to remember that examiners mark up (or down) from the pass mark. The pass mark represents two-thirds of the maximum mark.

The remarks will be written in a constructive way as far as is possible, but the examiner cannot in the short time available provide a full critique of the performances and will therefore give a general, overall impression with particular reference to a good point, or something that needs special attention. It is unlikely that this will deal with details of technique unless the performance has been affected adversely by any fundamental weakness; e.g. poor stance or idiosyncratic approach which will be detrimental to future development. Technical detail is a matter for the teacher to deal with within the pupil's overall progress. The examination assesses the candidate's achievement, not potential. It is not intended to be another lesson.

TOWARDS A PROFESSIONAL CAREER

It is important to remember that high marks gained in the upper grades do not automatically destine the candidate for a professional musical career. The required degree of maturity and understanding, plus the rigorous disciplines involved, are not part of the marking system in these examinations. Nevertheless, any candidate who has used the step-ladder intelligently and successfully will emerge at the end with a sound basis on which to pursue further studies at a more advanced level.

A FEW GENERAL THOUGHTS FOR TEACHERS

There can be no comparison between an examination and any other performance. You and your colleagues may have given your pupil a trial run and this can be extremely helpful, or your pupil may have played at a festival or a pupils' concert and received a very encouraging report. But no two live performances will ever be exactly the same and we all know that pupils can react in many different ways in examinations.

Needless to say the examiner can only comment on what s/he has heard at the examination. The remarks may well underline what you have been telling your pupil, or they may bring to light problems which have not previously been highlighted in lessons. This means that the marks and remarks on the mark form must be treated as an impartial assessment of what has been heard in the examination performance and the response to tests, based on the Associated Board's marking criteria. The marks will indicate the merit of the performance, but it may happen that the comments ignore some aspects of the playing of which you would be justly proud.

On the other hand the assessment cannot take into account the bad cold, the cut finger, the high temperature. It may also be thoughtless to pass around germs in the waiting room. The examiner will be sympathetic, but must assess work entirely on its own merits. Similarly, the examiner, although very helpful and sympathetic to candidates with special needs, will assess purely on musical achievement.

It is worth pointing out here that there is a scheme of Braille reading tests for blind candidates, and partially-sighted candidates may opt to take tests in large notation or aural repetition. For candidates with hearing impairment, special aural tests are available and guidelines have been established for the examination of dyslexic candidates.

NERVES

Nearly every candidate suffers from nerves in some form or another. Some will cope better than others. We all understand these feelings, as most of us have had to control anxiety when we took examinations ourselves. To have a secure technical control of the instrument can be one way of focusing attention on the music rather than on oneself.

Candidates should be encouraged to play to one another as often as possible. For pianists, safe and assured scale playing can be helpful for getting used to the touch of the unfamiliar piano at the start of the examination. This will lead to greater control of the keyboard and concentration on the task of performing.

PIANOS

The Associated Board makes every effort to ensure that the piano to be used is in satisfactory condition: not just adequate, but capable of producing sufficient sensitivity to help a deserving candidate gain Distinction at Grade 8. Examiners always try out the instrument before starting the session and if there is a fault it is dealt with as quickly as possible. Grand pianos may seem bewildering to children who are used to uprights so it is wise if pupils can be given the opportunity to play a grand piano prior to the examination, especially noting the different height of the music desk. On the other hand, uprights can be inhibiting to the advanced performer. In this situation it is hoped that candidates will realise that it is impossible to have grand pianos at all the thousands of centres where the Board examines.

DATE OF EXAMINATIONS

Understandably teachers often have a preference for examination dates. Because in planning a tour it is not possible to accommodate every wish, the Special Visits scheme was introduced in the UK to guarantee nearly any chosen day in the year. The examiner will visit the house or school as long as there are 5 hours of examinations. Teachers may of course join together to make up this amount of time. Another advantage of this scheme is that pupils will be familiar with the piano. In other countries the national or local administrator will encounter similar planning problems. Appreciating the logistics involved will help to understand why it is impossible for the Associated Board to respond to all requests, but requests for special dates will be considered sympathetically.

THE EXAMINATION ITSELF

Always check the requirements in the current syllabus and make sure you have selected the correct combination of pieces, otherwise the candidate may be penalised.

If you are entering a group of candidates it is suggested that you work out times for your pupils so that each can arrive 10 minutes before the time due, other considerations permitting. This will help to avoid a long and anxious wait for those at the end of your list. Make sure that pupils know what to expect, especially in the early grades, for instance, that they are familiar with the various types of aural test question. Tell them what to look for in the sight-reading and what to try out: so many children simply stare blankly at the music.

ACCOMPANISTS

Give instrumental candidates as much practice as possible in playing with the accompanist, and ensure that the pianist knows the correct tempo and will not overpower the soloist. If you yourself are wary of tackling the more difficult accompaniments or duo sonatas in the upper grades, it is wise to use a competent and reliable pianist. It is important that this suggestion is taken with candidates' best interests in mind. It makes the examiner's task very difficult if the pianist falters badly or plays too slowly, resulting, for instance, in bowing or breathing difficulties for the candidate.

THE END RESULT

It is important to remember that in the same way that it is unlikely that your teaching will deviate from a certain standard when instructing your pupils, the examiner's perception of what is expected will remain constant for all candidates. If the results are to you surprisingly low (or high), the candidates will almost invariably be the cause as they are inexperienced and react positively, negatively or indifferently to the situation. Some children will be good candidates; others will always react with less assurance. The Associated Board's thorough training and regular check on examiners' assessment procedures are designed to minimise discrepancies in marking standards.

SOME THOUGHTS FOR PARENTS

Examinations are designed to offer a framework for a progressive musical training providing periodic, impartial assessment. Marking is as objective as possible, in accordance with long-established criteria.

If your child needs encouragement solely through praise it may not be wise to enter them for examinations. The assessment will undoubtedly contain some criticism. It is the examiner's aim to be constructive in the report, but if the candidate is ill-prepared or unable to cope with the demands of the examination the examiner must refer to this if the examination is to have any value. In this respect the criteria explained on pages 28-32 will help you understand what is expected.

Paradoxically, the most conscientious children will often be the most nervous, as it will matter so much to them that they play well. This can lead to tension, and even cause a breakdown in a piece which they know very well. It is important, therefore, that parents do not put undue pressure on their children. Help them to relax and treat the occasion as an opportunity to give pleasure. Whatever the result, it should be accepted without recrimination to ensure a build-up of confidence for the future. If you sit in the waiting room and your child bursts into tears when the examination is over, do not automatically assume that it was the examiner's fault. Usually it is simply a release of tension. A child may have been composed and calm whilst playing and indeed performed well. Remember your composure will be the greatest help to the young musician. A calm, well prepared, unflustered candidate will usually do well. Therefore do not fuss unnecessarily. If you do, this will only increase anxiety and apprehension.

A frequent cause of failure is due to the pieces having been learnt over a long period of time with a subsequent loss of interest. If the same grade is to be retaken, it is wise to start new pieces otherwise nine months or more could have been spent in practising the same music with disastrous results for the child's love of music.

It is unwise to insist that your child takes an examination if there is resistance from the child, or if it would be against the teacher's advice. If forced to do so the result is likely to be disappointing, and any enjoyment in music-making will vanish.

The final paragraph in the section addressed to candidates (page 12) is important. Should your child want to have a career in music, it is important to have expert professional advice and this can usually be arranged through the teacher.

GENERAL HINTS FOR CANDIDATES

PRACTICAL EXAMINATIONS

It is a good idea to have your music ready before you enter the examination room. If you are not a pianist, take your instrument out of its case in the waiting room and make what preparations are necessary.

If you are a string player, someone may help you with tuning up to and including Grade 5, but you must do this yourself from Grade 6 upwards. Remember to carry spare strings in your case and a spare reed if you are a woodwind player. Make certain that your instrument is in good working condition prior to the examination, so that any fault may be put right in time.

If you are a wind player, warm up your instrument by blowing silently through it in the waiting room as this will help you to play better. However, take as much time as you need to tune up correctly. This is very important and also applies to string players.

Be ready to tell the examiner what you are going to play. If you think that you may forget, write down the names of your pieces. If you are playing a piece with a difficult page turn, you may photocopy the extra page, but you are not allowed to play a whole piece from a photocopy as it is illegal unless you have permission in writing from the publisher. Do not ask the examiner to turn over for you: the examiner might be writing at the time when you were expecting a page to be turned.

The examiner will always be listening, even if s/he does not appear to be doing so. Sometimes s/he will miss a break to avoid keeping candidates waiting, and have coffee and a biscuit during an examination – please do not be surprised or offended by this. It may also be necessary to stop you during a longer piece, but be assured s/he will have heard sufficient to have formed an impression of how you play and how well you have prepared your performances. If the examiner asks for a scale, or an aural test, which seems unfamiliar, do not be afraid to say so. It is much easier to correct an error at once, should there be a mistake.

And, lastly, when examiners are being trained or moderated it is necessary for them to work together, so do not be put off if two people are present: only one will be marking your performance.

(See also section on Examiners page 20.)

WRITTEN EXAMINATIONS

Do not forget to bring a selection of pens and pencils with you.

Make sure that you read each question carefully and understand what is needed. If a question has several different parts, you might find it easier to tick off each part as you complete it – that way you will not miss any.

Write your answers neatly and clearly on the printed question paper. If you need to do some rough work first, you should use the manuscript paper which is provided for you.

Always check through your paper before leaving the examination room and make sure you have answered all the questions.

It is a good idea to work through some sample papers before the examination so that you get used to working within a time limit. It will also prepare you for the sort of questions you will get in the examination itself.

THE EXAMINER - THE PERSON BEHIND THE TABLE

The Associated Board has about 600 examiners on its panel and this number will continue to rise in order to meet the demands for the Board's examinations worldwide. Examiners are chosen very carefully and will already be respected in the world of music: they will have had experience in teaching and working with pupils at all levels. Apart from their own considerable expertise, the Board looks for a kind, pleasant, sympathetic personality to bring out the best in a candidate. Examiners will understand anxiety, and know how best to deal with a timid child or nervous adult, and above all will be fair. There is no such thing as a severe examiner. It is important that candidates remember this fact. So much damage can be done through hearsay and gossip, not least that which is generated in the waiting room where, added to the general apprehension, the examiner becomes a dreaded figure who sits at a table and who never smiles. This is a great pity, since all examiners want to be helpful and would not be doing the job if that were not the case.

Some are naturally friendly and outgoing, and others are quieter and more reserved. Above all, they want candidates to play (or sing) at their best, and would much rather give praise than criticism.

The training to become an examiner is very thorough. It involves the initial training, when the procedures and marking schemes are learnt, followed by practice-examining with "volunteer" candidates. Then comes an opportunity to sit in on "real" examinations to observe good practice. After this begins a period of direction of examinations under expert guidance. When the Chief Examiner is satisfied that a new examiner is ready, their name will be recommended to the Board's Governing Body for placement on the panel of examiners. But that is not the end of training, for all examiners have to attend regular in-service seminars and are routinely moderated to ensure standards are maintained.

The in-service seminars are directed by specialists who discuss the marking assessment of "volunteer" candidates with emphasis placed on what should or should not be possible at the different grade levels. The technical problems involved in playing various instruments are illustrated, also the degree of musicianship which can be expected in the early grades.

Whenever possible, examinations are conducted by specialists at Advanced Certificate level and at LRSM diploma level.

It will be seen from the above that to be an examiner is not an easy job and that is why so much care is taken in the selection and training. Sir Hugh Allen, Director of the Royal College of Music from 1919 to 1937 once wrote:

"The technique, as far as I can see, of an Examiner of the Associated Board would be compounded of a talent for simple arithmetic, an elastic vocabulary, a synthetic memory, a decent handwriting, an unwearied patience, a ready power of description, a gentle demeanour, a sense of justice, solicitude for the weak, a taste for logic, a golden voice and a bedside manner."

The language might be dated, but the underlying message is as true today as it was sixty years ago.

FREQUENT QUERIES

Will the examiner help my pupil who has a breaking voice?
Yes, by finding the best range for the voice. Whistling and humming are acceptable alternatives.

Will any edition be acceptable?
Yes, we will accept any edition used, but the named editions in the syllabus will provide a useful guide.

How are pieces selected for the syllabus?
Very experienced teachers/performers are asked to select each syllabus. When finalised, an independent specialist moderates the material for the entire category (e.g wind, brass or strings) to ensure a similar standard overall.

How many scales will be asked?
Certainly not all of them, but sufficient to cover all the requirements of the grade.

Is the metronome mark important?
Up to a point, yes, for it will be more likely to lead to the correct style if the composer's intentions are followed. Where a metronome mark has not been provided by the composer it is likely that an editor will suggest a tempo – normally given within square brackets – and this, too, if followed, should help create the right style for the piece.

What happens if the examiner is running late?
This is difficult. It is often the candidate who dictates the speed of an examination. Examiners have to listen to scales and pieces played at the tempo chosen by the candidate. Sight-reading is also played at the candidate's tempo, and aural responses have to be given before the next test is started. The examiner will not cut short an examination in order to catch up, but will make every endeavour to keep to the timetable.

Do examiners have to pass or fail a certain percentage of candidates?

No. Assessment is entirely based on the achievement of the individual candidate using the published criteria. It is therefore possible for all candidates to pass or, conversely, fail, if the standard for a Pass is not achieved.

Isn't it unfair to fail a Grade 1 candidate, as it is the first exam?

No one likes failing a candidate, but the pass standard must start somewhere. The Preparatory Test is helpful, as it has no Pass or Fail. It prepares the candidate for the standard required at Grade 1 and provides valuable experience in coping with the examination situation.

Is there an age limit for entry?

All Associated Board examinations (except the Performance Assessment) are open to candidates of all ages. Examiners do not take age into consideration in any assessment.

What provision does the Associated Board make for candidates with special needs?

The Associated Board is anxious to provide opportunity for all candidates irrespective of any physical, learning or sensory difficulties. Details of alternative examination tests are given on page 13.

In all cases candidates are expected (and indeed wish) to be assessed according to the same criteria.

Additionally, the Performance Assessment scheme is open to candidates of all ages who have learning difficulties which make the graded examinations an inappropriate option.

RECOMMENDED MINIMUM SPEEDS FOR SCALES AND ARPEGGIOS

Please refer to the piano, woodwind and brass scale books published by the Associated Board for further information.

PIANO

	Scales	Broken chords and arpeggios
Grade 1	♩ = 60	♩. = 46
Grade 2	♩ = 66	♩ = 63
Grade 3	♩ = 80	♩ = 69
Grade 4	𝅗𝅥 = 52	♩ = 76
Grade 5	𝅗𝅥 = 63	♩ = 88
Grade 6	𝅗𝅥 = 76	𝅗𝅥 = 50
Grade 7	𝅗𝅥 = 80	𝅗𝅥 = 56
Grade 8	𝅗𝅥 = 88	𝅗𝅥 = 66

WOODWIND AND BRASS Major and minor scales, chromatic scales, scales in thirds, whole-tone scales, dominant and diminished sevenths

	Woodwind and Brass valved instruments (excluding horn)	Horn	Trombone
Grade 1	♩ = 50	♩ = 50	♩ = 44
Grade 2	♩ = 56	♩ = 56	♩ = 48
Grade 3	♩ = 66	♩ = 66	♩ = 56
Grade 4	♩ = 72	♩ = 72	♩ = 63
Grade 5	♩ = 80	♩ = 80	♩ = 72
Grade 6	♩ = 104	♩ = 96	♩ = 96
Grade 7	♩ = 116	♩ = 108	♩ = 108
Grade 8	♩ = 132	♩ = 120	♩ = 120

WOODWIND AND BRASS	Major and minor arpeggios		
	Woodwind and Brass valved instruments (excluding horn)	Horn	Trombone
Grade 1	♪ = 72	♪ = 72	♪ = 66
Grade 2	♪ = 80	♪ = 80	♪ = 72
Grade 3	♪ = 92	♪ = 92	♪ = 84
Grade 4	♪ = 100	♪ = 100	♪ = 92
Grade 5	♪ = 112	♪ = 112	♪ = 104
Grade 6	♩. = 56	♩. = 56	♩. = 46
Grade 7	♩. = 66	♩. = 66	♩. = 56
Grade 8	♩. = 76	♩. = 76	♩. = 60

Breathing should be incorporated where possible to maintain line, and should certainly not be used as a means to negotiate the break or octave.

STRINGS

Bowing will dictate the tempi of slurred scales and arpeggios for strings. Scales and arpeggios with separate bows should be brisk, using no more than half the bow length.

Guitarists should start scales ♩ = 90 at Grade 1, increasing to ♩ = 186 by Grade 4, then two notes to each beat = 120 by Grade 5, increasing to two notes to each beat = 166 by Grade 8.

EXAMINATIONS STRUCTURE AND CRITERIA FOR ASSESSMENT

GUIDING PRINCIPLES IN PRACTICAL EXAMINATIONS

a) Technical accomplishment: accuracy, facility, co-ordination, physical and instrumental control (e.g. breathing, bowing etc).

b) Musical understanding: the quality of interpretation, responding to the inherent style and structure of the music including sensitivity to tonal quality, phrasing, articulation, melodic and rhythmic shape.

c) Communication: the ability to convey the meaning and spirit of the music, the joy and innate awareness of the art of performance as conveyed to the listener.

BASIS OF ASSESSMENT: THE RELATIONSHIP BETWEEN EXAMINER AND CANDIDATE

All assessment depends upon the extent of the success, as illustrated by the candidate in the examination, in reaching and fulfilling the required criteria. Since all members of the panel have been similarly trained to assess to these criteria, stability of marking standards can be ensured.

Candidates' skills are tested by performing three pieces, or more, as required in the syllabus, plus illustrating technique in scales or exercises. Aural perception is also tested, and ability to perform at sight.

Examiners' comments, written during the examination, are matched by corresponding marks, and are based upon the criteria as detailed below.

All marking is from a pass mark of 66%. Grades for the purpose of criteria are broadly banded as follows:

Grades 1 – 4   primarily the establishment of good practice i.e. technical accuracy with some evidence of musical feeling.

Grade 5   an intermediate stage where musicality becomes a more important element.

Grades 6 and 7   in which technical security and a sense of performance can be expected.

Grade 8   in which stylistic awareness, musical sensitivity and technical competence are evident and interdependent.

Total marks in all graded practical examinations are 150. 100 marks are required to achieve a Pass, 120 marks to pass with Merit and 130 marks to pass with Distinction.

A certificate is awarded to all candidates who have reached the standard required to pass. Marks are not included on the certificate. The certificate will indicate the category of pass.

PIECES

The table on pages 28-29 illustrates the basis of marking within the broad bands. Each piece will be assessed independently using the principle of marking from the pass mark (negatively or positively) with reference to the requirement for a pass mark. Marks will be awarded according to the extent of the competence within the range of marks.

Marks within brackets apply when there are 3 pieces with a maximum of 30 marks each. A similar but proportionally adjusted range applies in singing examinations.

	Grades 1-4	Grade 5
Distinction *(26 - 30)*	Technical fluency Ability to let the music speak A confident performance	Technical fluency Musically aware and expressive Ability to communicate the feeling of the music
Merit *(24 - 26)*	Good sense of rhythm A high level of technical security Evidence of instrumental/vocal control (e.g. sustained tone, breathing, bowing distribution) Awareness of phrase shape and balance Attention to dynamic requirements	A high level of technical security Developing instrumental/vocal competence (e.g. pedalling, vibrato where appropriate) Well-judged tempi, phrasing/articulation Demonstration of tonal qualities (e.g. cantabile playing)
Pass *(20 - 23)*	Grasp of rhythm General accuracy of notes and intonation Adequate though limited musical interest Evidence of careful preparation	Fair sense of rhythm Broadly accurate Suitable and sustained tempo Developing dynamic range Some recognition of style including attention to phrasing/articulation
Below Pass standard *(19 and under)*	Failure to grasp rhythm Careless note placing and/or intonation Lack of continuity (e.g. searching for notes) Fluctuating tempo Devoid of musical interest	Imprecise rhythm Careless note playing Loss of tempo at points of difficulty Lack of concern for dynamic variety Omission of phrasing/articulation detail

Grades 6-7	Grade 8
Technical fluency Musically committed interpretation Imaginative and instinctive quality of communication	Fluent and authoritative playing/singing Musically convincing and aesthetically satisfying performance
A high level of technical security Skilful use of instrumental/vocal techniques Good sense of musical style Effective use of tonal qualities	A high level of technical security and instrumental/vocal control Highly sensitive use of tonal qualities (e.g. gradation and variety of tone, timbre, colour) Strong stylistic characteristics
Overall accuracy Appropriate tempi and dynamics Adequate stylistic understanding, including pedalling and vibrato where appropriate	Overall accuracy Sensitivity to instrumental/vocal tone Stylistic awareness
Technical insecurity Loss of continuity through inappropriate choice of tempo Inadequate stylistic concept	Technical insecurity Misapplication of instrumental/vocal techniques Absence of musical imagination

SUPPORTING TESTS

Scales, arpeggios and technical exercises: a progressive development of essential instrumental and vocal skills.

A similar scheme of marking is applied appropriate to the grade. The pass mark is 14: the maximum mark is 21.

	All Grades
(19 – 21)	Quick response
	Technically fluent and effortless
	Musically shaped
(17 – 18)	Ready response
	Well prepared
	Technically secure
	Evidence of flair
(14 – 16)	Cautious response
	Adequately prepared
	Moderate tempo
	Some technical unevenness
Below Pass standard: *(13 and under)*	Poor response
	Sporadic and uneven playing
	Very slow tempo
	Technically insecure

SIGHT-READING

The Associated Board publishes specimen sight-reading tests in all subjects for all grades. These illustrate the gradual, but increasing difficulties which candidates will be required to face. Organ candidates and some brass candidates additionally undertake a transposition test at Grades 6, 7 and 8. The examiner allows half a minute for silent or performed preparation according to the wishes of the candidate before the assessment begins. As with scales, arpeggios and technical exercises, the pass mark is 14: the maximum mark is 21.

	All Grades
(19 – 21)	Fluent
	Attention to expressive details
	Musically aware
(17 – 18)	Mostly accurate
	Steady pulse
	Appropriate tempo
(14 – 16)	Broadly accurate
	Generally steady pulse
	Awareness of key
Below Pass standard:	Poor recognition of time and notes
(13 and under)	Lack of continuity
	Disregard for key

AURAL TESTS

The Associated Board publishes specimen tests for all grades. All candidates take the same group of tests. These are carefully graded from basic recognition of rhythm and memory of short phrases to tests demanding well-developed aural perception and discrimination. The pass mark is 12: the maximum mark is 18.

	All Grades
(18)	Quick and perceptive response
(15 – 17)	Good response
	Minor errors or hesitation
(12 – 14)	An adequate response
	Some hesitation and error
Below Pass standard:	Slow response
(11 and under)	Inaccuracy in majority of tests

ENSEMBLE

The Associated Board has an ensemble syllabus which is designed to encourage practising musicians to make music together without direction.

Requirements: Groups comprising any reasonable combination of two to eight performers with one person to each part may enter for examination. This includes duos consisting of an instrumentalist and a keyboard player where both performers wish to be assessed as an ensemble, and piano duets.

Levels of assessment: Primary: for ensembles approaching the standard required in Grades 4 – 5.

Intermediate: for ensembles of approximately Grades 6 – 7 standard.

Advanced: for ensembles of approximately Grade 8 standard.

Pieces: All groups will be required to play two items, contrasted in style and tempo, chosen either from the suggested lists of works (given simply as a guideline to expected standards) or from any other works, published or unpublished, of the group's own choice which are similar in standard and have serious musical aims, provided a score has been submitted to the Associated Board for approval one month prior to the date of entry.

Assessment: The examiner will award a grade, rather than a mark, for each of the two items offered. This grade will take into account the following elements of the performance:

1) Technical competence (including ensemble, balance and intonation).

2) Texture (including unanimity of outlook, detail, contrast and blend).

3) Interpretation (including rhythmic sense, phrasing, choice of tempi and attention to marks of expression).

An overall mark based on these two gradings will then be awarded. The gradings will be as follows:

A: an outstanding performance with little reservation,

B: a very good performance, but with some reservation,

C: a competent performance, but with significant reservation,

F: failure to reach the standard required to pass.

Plus may be added to grades A, B and C, and minus to A and B.

ADVANCED CERTIFICATE

In 1990, following extensive consultation with teachers in schools, colleges, universities, the private sector and specialist organisations, an Advanced Certificate was introduced as an intermediate step between Grade 8 and diploma level, and indeed it is an essential prequalification for entry to the LRSM diploma.

The assessment is in two parts. The first is a recital of between 20 and 40 minutes according to subject and the second consists of a quick study test and a viva voce including musicianship tests and questions on repertoire. The assessment will be conducted by a specialist examiner wherever practicable. Each section will be graded as follows:

A: an outstanding performance,

B: a good performance,

C: an acceptable performance,

F: failure to reach the standard required to pass.

Plus or minus may be added to grades A, B and C.

An overall grade will not be awarded. Candidates will be required to obtain a minimum C grading in both sections in the same examination session to be awarded the Advanced Certificate. Candidates gaining an A grading in both sections will be awarded the Certificate with Distinction.

LICENTIATE DIPLOMA

The Licentiate of the Royal Schools of Music is equivalent in standard to the diploma of LRAM conferred by the Royal Academy of Music and the ARCM conferred by the Royal College of Music, and receives equal recognition.

The LRSM syllabus ensures that diploma holders have a broad base of musicianship, whatever their chosen specialism. Having achieved the Advanced Certificate prequalification, applicants go on to a common Part 1 comprising two papers, the first of which tests aural awareness and knowledge of the theory of music (the latter at about Grade 8 level). The second is concerned with applied musical knowledge, and includes questions on repertoire which assume a basic background knowledge of music from 1500 to the present day as well as more specialised knowledge of a range of options, and questions on instrumental or vocal techniques.

Having achieved a Pass at Part 1, candidates move on to Part 2, opting for one of six Branches: Composition; Music in the School Curriculum; Teaching (Instrumental or Voice); Performance; Direction

(Bandmastership, Choral Conducting or Orchestral Conducting); Piano Accompaniment. All of these involve an extended viva voce, and some additionally require written work, either in the form of a portfolio or case studies, and – for teachers – a further written paper.

An overall grade is not awarded. Candidates who have demonstrated an appropriate level of professional competence are awarded a Pass. Those who are not successful have the opportunity of retaking those modules of the diploma at which they were unsuccessful.

PREPARATORY TEST

This is a test designed to offer an independent assessment normally at the end of the first year's tuition. The assessment is therefore confined to the recording of a pupil's achievement to date. It is not marked, or graded, according to criteria. A helpful written report is given to the candidate at the end of the test.

PERFORMANCE ASSESSMENT

The Performance Assessment is a scheme introduced in 1993 which enables any musician aged 21 or over to have their prepared work assessed by a member of the Associated Board's examining panel, and to receive a constructive, written report which is handed to them at the end of the assessment by the examiner. There is no Pass or Fail.

There is an entirely free choice of repertoire, the only stipulation being that the programme should last no more than 15 minutes.

There are no supporting tests, and the aim is to remove much of the pressure normally associated with examinations or public performance so that the musician can concentrate on his or her performance without fear of failure.

The assessment is appropriate to any level of achievement, and adult beginners should find it as useful as advanced level performers. It may also be used by teachers who want a confidential assessment of their playing as part of their continuing professional development.

(See also page 23 regarding candidates with special needs.)

PRACTICAL MUSICIANSHIP

This syllabus is designed for assessment of musicianship. Instrumentalists and singers are able to choose the medium they use to respond to a number of tests ranging in difficulty from basic musical responses at Grade 1 level to advanced musicianship tasks, including free and structured improvisation, at Grade 8.

Assessment at all grades will be by means of a written report and grading:

A: a Pass with Distinction,

B: a Pass with Merit,

C: a Pass,

F: failure to reach the standard required to pass.

Plus may be added to grades A, B and C, and minus to A and B.

THEORY OF MUSIC

It is the belief of the Associated Board that there is still a place for a thorough knowledge of the elements of music and that at some stage in the instrumentalist's and singer's development these should be tested, not least because they provide a foundation for later independence in musical performance.

For this reason the Associated Board requires a pass at Grade 5 in Theory (or Practical Musicianship) as part of the higher practical grade examinations (i.e. Grades 6 – 8). There is no time limit to the validity of the theory qualification.

Assessment is by written examination marked according to a common marking scheme. Marks are awarded out of a maximum of 100. A minimum of 66 is required to pass, 90 for a pass with Distinction. Normal moderation and sampling procedures are used to maintain standards in the setting of questions and uniformity in their marking.